MW00344116

the BREAD BAKER'S NOTEBOOK

_____

_____

PRINCETON ARCHITECTURAL PRESS · NEW YORK

There are many ways to learn to bake bread. Books. Websites. Videos. (So many videos!) Perhaps someone's gifted you sourdough starter or their favorite recipe. But the best teacher of bread baking is your own history with it. If you keep a record of your successes and failures, the bread will teach you how to bake better bread. Failure can be a beautiful process.

It's a personal victory to make bread. You are interacting with yourself, the weather, a food infrastructure, your body chemistry, the air. Your science brain. Your math brain. Your hands and your humanity. Your community. To make bread is to use the past to create something for the future.

Do you know how kids (and adults) of a certain age like making slime, and they become so proficient at it that they start selling it? Slime started out as a tool for self-regulation. Baking bread is slime for adults. The touching. The mixing. The pulling. Getting to know your dough is a mental escape from stress that also provides breakfast.

If you bake with a sourdough starter, then you are using a mother. The mother. The mother you feed and care for. The tables seem turned—until your mother provides. When life feels unmanageable or sad, caring for something outside yourself feels like self-care.

Bread making is a sequence of relatively short actions interspersed with periods of waiting. Baking is an endless repetition of weighing, measuring, mixing, and waiting. You

organize your day around baking, or you make it fit into your schedule. There is the kneading, dividing, and shaping. Opening the oven. Closing it. Opening it again. Taking your bread out. Cleaning your floor, your countertops, your tools. Above all, your hands. Wondering what you did wrong.

It's important to spread projects over days, so you wake up in anticipation of the next step. Bread baking gives you a reason to rise. Bread is therapy. It's also an obligation. It needs you; you knead it.

You make bread to eat with cheese. You make bread for toast. You make bread to give it away. You make it to help someone feel better. Someone had a nightmare. Their dad is sick. They need bread. They have dentures—they need soft bread. The stories make the bread. The bread makes the stories.

What kind of baker are you? The baker in quarantine who ripped out their first loaves like a pro? The baker who understands science? The baker who does it for the story? The baker who doesn't like to follow instructions? The baker who is somewhat annoyed that baking bread has become so popular? The baker who never thought they could bake?

Life is fragile. Bread is not. Pay close attention to your bread, and it will teach you everything you need to know.

AUTOLYZE: when you combine flour and water and let the mixture sit for a while before adding salt, yeast, or leaven. This process starts the gluten formation, makes for a smoother dough, and cuts down on your mixing time later on. It is not necessary for great bread, but some bakers find it adds flavor and longevity.

BULK FERMENTATION: baby's first big rise. Scientifically, what's happening here is that the yeast is eating the carbs and farting out carbon dioxide, aided by a series of stretches and folds. It's called bulk because the dough is all together. It hasn't been separated into loaves and left its family yet.

DISCARD: if you are using a sourdough starter, is the quantity of starter you do not use; if you are feeding your starter, the amount you take out just before. Rather than get rid of it, as the name suggests, collect it in a jar. There are countless uses for discard. Discarding keeps your mother nice and refreshed and avoids accumulation of an unwieldy amount of starter.

FOLDING: a technique that aids in the building of the gluten structure. During bulk fermentation pull up the dough and fold it over in the bowl, turning the bowl as you go.

GLUTEN: the proteins found in some grains (wheat, spelt, and rye, for example). When broken down and fermented with water, salt, and a leavening agent, it binds together and accounts for the elasticity in the dough.

LEAVEN (*also called preferment, levain*): a small amount of sourdough with more flour and water added in, left to sit for a few hours before mixing.

OVEN SPRING: a beautiful madness that is the last rise for your dough. It generally takes place halfway through your bake, and it can be a vindication of all your work, a mirror of your mistakes, or pure magic. You could have great oven spring—a giant, bouncing loaf—or you could have sad flatness. Keeping a log will help you figure out what led you to greatness.

OVERPROOFING AND UNDERPROOFING:
Your bread will let you know something went wrong. Maybe it's become a flat, delicious slipper. Or full of holes. Figuring out what went awry may take some sleuthing. If you haven't let your bread proof long enough, it won't be strong enough to rise. If you overproofed your bread, the beautiful air inside the dough has escaped. This is the quagmire for new bakers, and you will flail about here for sure. Rejoice in your mistakes. They build your muscles.

PROOFING: your bread's final rise, after shaping. Some people do this in the refrigerator—a cold proof.

RETARDING: placing your bread in a colder environment to slow down the yeast fermentation. It's like pressing pause.

SCORING: slashing with a razor once your bread is ready to be baked. The purpose of scoring is to help the dough expand during its oven spring. Many bakers flex their muscles here and make beautiful, intricate designs. (There are innumerable examples on Instagram.)

SHAPING: the next step after bulk fermentation. Shape the dough into the loaf of your dreams, either in a bowl or on a work surface. Shaped dough goes into a basket to help it keep the shape. There are numerous ASMR videos online of bakers shaping to keep you soothed for hours.

SOURDOUGH STARTER (*also called the mother*): this is your wild yeast. If you are baking sourdough bread, the starter is your first key to the kingdom.

SPONGE: a bit of flour, water, and yeast set to rise before you mix in the main ingredients. It creates a fermented taste somewhat like sourdough but in much less time.

YEAST: a leavening agent. If you do not care to capture your own wild yeast culture, you can buy one at the grocery store. Commercially made yeast makes your bread rise pretty rapidly. There is active dry, instant, and fresh yeast.

WHEAT: many types of flour are made from this grain; there are many kinds. The wheat kernel contains endosperm, germ, and bran.

FLOUR: grain kernels ground to a powder in a mill. There are many different kinds of flour, each with a unique flavor, texture, and protein content.

ALL-PURPOSE FLOUR: ground-up endosperm of a blend of wheats; used for breads, pizza, cookies, and pastries.

BREAD FLOUR: flour with a high protein content, specifically for bread baking.

RYE FLOUR: a nutritious flour ground from rye berries. Often used in sourdough starters, it has a distinct flavor.

WHOLE WHEAT FLOUR: ground from an entire wheat grain, without sifting out the bran and germ.

SPECIALTY GRAINS: emmer, spelt, and einkorn are just a few of the many grains ground into flours and used in addition to bread flour or all-purpose flour for baking.

SMALL-BATCH MILLING: grinding one's own flours using home mills and berries—hence the term "freshly milled."

S coring, or cutting the bread just before you bake it, helps control which way the air escapes. If you don't score it, you'll get a natural fault line, and that's beautiful too. If you want to make a nice traditional design, there are demonstrations of wheat stalks and other cuts on the internet to peruse, try, and fail to reproduce. Don't ram your knife or blade too far down. If you go at an angle, you'll get a nice curve.

You can ruin your loaf with a bad scoring job, which is a lot of pressure. You can buy a fancy tool for it or go low-tech and attach a double-sided razor blade to a coffee stirrer.

A starter, or the mother, is where life begins for sourdough bread. It has two ingredients: flour and water. You can make it yourself or get some from a friend. Keep it in a clear glass container, so you can see it rising and falling. As you learn to care for it, you will understand when to use it for bread making. It rises and is ready for use just before it starts to fall.

If you do not plan to bake several times a week, you can keep your starter in the refrigerator. A starter can live for weeks there in a dormant state, and it only needs to be taken out, brought to room temperature, and fed to come back to life.

Making sourdough bread generates a fair amount of excess starter. Each time you refresh or feed your starter, you take out a bit. Too much mother? Make pancakes. Crepes. Waffles. Banana bread. It's a perfect, soothing system. A wasteless project you can share with others.

SOURDOUGH STARTER LOG: EXPLAINED

DATE OF BIRTH

What day and month did you start your starter?

STARTER NAME

Some people name their starters. It's especially useful if you have two or more.

FLOUR TYPE

What kind of flour did you use to build your starter?

RATIO OF FLOUR TO WATER

How much are you feeding your starter?

STARTER LOCATION   Where does your starter live?

○ *Fridge*   ○ *Counter*   ○ *Other* _____

FEEDING SCHEDULE   If you keep your starter outside the fridge, how often do you feed it?

S	*M*	*T*	*W*	*H*	*F*	*S*

BREAD LOG: EXPLAINED

DATE

Note this because once you start baking bread
regularly, the loaves all look alike.

RECIPE

What recipe are you working with?

SEASON ○ Winter ○ Spring ○ Summer ○ Fall

WEATHER ○ Rainy ○ Foggy ○ Humid ○ Dry ○ Sunny

Kitchen temperature: _____   *Outside temperature:* _____

Temperature, both outside your house and in your kitchen, greatly affects your bake. If it's very
humid, your bread will rise faster. If it's cold, it might need more time.

YOUR MOOD

How are you feeling?

YOUR STARTER'S MOOD

How is you starter looking?

STARTER   What starter and what yeast type are you using? When did you last feed
it? You'll start to notice the optimum time to use your starter.

Amount of starter (in grams): _____   *Amount of leaven, if using (in grams):* _____

TYPES AND AMOUNTS OF FLOUR (IN GRAMS)

Different flours will impact the taste and texture of your bread, so play around beyond basic
white flour. Spelt, rye, or whole wheat might work for your regular loaf. Whole grains tend
to cook faster and have more nutrients.

WATER

This is very important. Many people use warm water for bread baking.

Temperature: _____   *Total amount of water:* _____

TOTAL INGREDIENT WEIGHT

IF MULTIPLE LOAVES, WEIGHT OF EACH

Knowing your dough's total weight in advance will be helpful if you are making multiple loaves
and want to divide it up.

TIME OF AUTOLYZE

The duration over which you let the flour and water sit prior to adding yeast or salt.

ADD-INS, IF USED   ◯ *Cheese*   ◯ *Raisins*   ◯ *Seeds*   ◯ *Nuts*   ◯ *Olives*

RESTING TIME

After you mix most of your ingredients together, let them get to know one another
a bit before you add the salt.

SALT

How much you added, and what kind.

KNEADING TIME   ◯ *No-Knead Bread*

After you mix your salt in, you are ready to knead your bread. Some people like to knead
their ingredients together, wait five minutes, then knead again. Use this space to note how
long you kneaded, and if you kneaded again after a rest.

STRETCHES AND FOLDS

How many folds: _____   *Time between:* _____

Stretch your bread up and fold it over a few times during bulk fermentation to build
tension in the dough and strengthen the gluten.

QUALITY OF DOUGH   ◯ *Sticky*   ◯ *Dry*   ◯ *Cohesive*   ◯ *Soupy*   ◯ *Clumpy*

How does your dough feel after the first mix? Sticky? Cohesive?
A soup you fear will never amount to anything?

BULK FERMENTATION TIME

The total time that you let your dough rise, undisturbed.

SHAPING, APPEARANCE, AND DOUGH TEXTURE BETWEEN STRETCHES AND FOLDS

There are various shaping techniques (and millions available to watch online).
Find one that you feel comfortable with, and repeat it many times.

RISE

How much did your bread rise while in the oven?

SCORING

Draw the shape of your score.

OVEN TEMPERATURE   You might preheat your oven to a hotter temperature than you will bake at. Whole grains brown faster and turn into sugar during fermentation. Think caramelization. If baking with whole-grain flours, consider lowering the initial oven temperature and then lowering the final temperature even more.

BAKING TIME

If baking with a covered pan, did you take off the lid?

With lid: _____   *Without lid:* _____

REFRIGERATOR TIME

How long did you put your bread in the fridge?

CRUST COLOR

Hard, burned, thin, thick?

BAKED LOAF CRUMB

What do the holes inside your bread look and feel like when you cut it open?

TASTE ⃝ Sour ⃝ Bland ⃝ Dry ⃝ Gummy ⃝ Perfect

WHO DID YOU GIVE YOUR BREAD TO? WHY?

Keep a record of who you gave bread to, what they thought of it, and why you gave it to them.

TO DO DIFFERENTLY NEXT TIME

SOURDOUGH STARTER LOG

DATE OF BIRTH

STARTER NAME

FLOUR TYPE

RATIO OF FLOUR TO WATER

STARTER LOCATION

◯ *Fridge*   ◯ *Counter*   ◯ *Other* _____

FEEDING SCHEDULE

S	*M*	*T*	*W*	*H*	*F*	*S*

SOURDOUGH STARTER LOG

DATE OF BIRTH

STARTER NAME

FLOUR TYPE

RATIO OF FLOUR TO WATER

STARTER LOCATION

○ *Fridge*   ○ *Counter*   ○ *Other*

FEEDING SCHEDULE

S	*M*	*T*	*W*	*H*	*F*	*S*

SOURDOUGH STARTER LOG

DATE OF BIRTH

STARTER NAME

FLOUR TYPE

RATIO OF FLOUR TO WATER

STARTER LOCATION

○ *Fridge*   ○ *Counter*   ○ *Other* _____

FEEDING SCHEDULE

S	*M*	*T*	*W*	*H*	*F*	*S*

SOURDOUGH STARTER LOG

DATE OF BIRTH

STARTER NAME

FLOUR TYPE

RATIO OF FLOUR TO WATER

STARTER LOCATION

◯ *Fridge*   ◯ *Counter*   ◯ *Other* _____

FEEDING SCHEDULE

S	*M*	*T*	*W*	*H*	*F*	*S*

Keep a jar in your fridge
for excess sourdough, and bake
with it at your leisure.

You can dry out
your sourdough starter and
give it away too.

Don't be scared to taste your starter. Just like touching it, smelling and tasting will tell you if the starter is too sour.

BREAD LOG

DATE

RECIPE

SEASON ◯ Winter ◯ Spring ◯ Summer ◯ Fall

WEATHER ◯ Rainy ◯ Foggy ◯ Humid ◯ Dry ◯ Sunny

Kitchen temperature: _____

Outside temperature: _____

YOUR MOOD

YOUR STARTER'S MOOD

STARTER

Amount of starter (in grams): _____

Amount of leaven, if using (in grams): _____

TYPES AND AMOUNTS OF FLOUR (IN GRAMS)

WATER

Temperature: _____

Total amount of water: _____

TOTAL INGREDIENT WEIGHT

IF MULTIPLE LOAVES, WEIGHT OF EACH

TIME OF AUTOLYZE

ADD-INS, IF USED   ◯ *Cheese*   ◯ *Raisins*   ◯ *Seeds*   ◯ *Nuts*   ◯ *Olives*

RESTING TIME

SALT

KNEADING TIME   ◯ *No-Knead Bread*

STRETCHES AND FOLDS

How many folds: _____   *Time between:* _____

QUALITY OF DOUGH   ◯ *Sticky*   ◯ *Dry*   ◯ *Cohesive*   ◯ *Soupy*   ◯ *Clumpy*

BULK FERMENTATION TIME

SHAPING, APPEARANCE, AND DOUGH TEXTURE BETWEEN STRETCHES AND FOLDS

RISE

SCORING

OVEN TEMPERATURE

BAKING TIME

With lid: _____   *Without lid:* _____

REFRIGERATOR TIME

CRUST COLOR

BAKED LOAF CRUMB

TASTE   ◯ *Sour*   ◯ *Bland*   ◯ *Dry*   ◯ *Gummy*   ◯ *Perfect*

WHO DID YOU GIVE YOUR BREAD TO? WHY?

TO DO DIFFERENTLY NEXT TIME

BREAD LOG

DATE

RECIPE

SEASON   ◯ *Winter*   ◯ *Spring*   ◯ *Summer*   ◯ *Fall*

WEATHER   ◯ *Rainy*   ◯ *Foggy*   ◯ *Humid*   ◯ *Dry*   ◯ *Sunny*

Kitchen temperature: _____

Outside temperature: _____

YOUR MOOD

YOUR STARTER'S MOOD

STARTER

Amount of starter (in grams): _____

Amount of leaven, if using (in grams): _____

TYPES AND AMOUNTS OF FLOUR (IN GRAMS)

WATER

Temperature: _____

Total amount of water: _____

TOTAL INGREDIENT WEIGHT

IF MULTIPLE LOAVES, WEIGHT OF EACH

TIME OF AUTOLYZE

ADD-INS, IF USED ◯ *Cheese* ◯ *Raisins* ◯ *Seeds* ◯ *Nuts* ◯ *Olives*

RESTING TIME

SALT

KNEADING TIME ◯ *No-Knead Bread*

STRETCHES AND FOLDS

How many folds: _____ *Time between:* _____

QUALITY OF DOUGH ◯ *Sticky* ◯ *Dry* ◯ *Cohesive* ◯ *Soupy* ◯ *Clumpy*

BULK FERMENTATION TIME

SHAPING, APPEARANCE, AND DOUGH TEXTURE BETWEEN STRETCHES AND FOLDS

RISE

SCORING

OVEN TEMPERATURE

BAKING TIME

With lid: _____   *Without lid:* _____

REFRIGERATOR TIME

CRUST COLOR

BAKED LOAF CRUMB

TASTE   ◯ *Sour*   ◯ *Bland*   ◯ *Dry*   ◯ *Gummy*   ◯ *Perfect*

WHO DID YOU GIVE YOUR BREAD TO? WHY?

TO DO DIFFERENTLY NEXT TIME

BREAD LOG

_____   _____
DATE   RECIPE

_____
SEASON   ◯ Winter   ◯ Spring   ◯ Summer   ◯ Fall
WEATHER   ◯ Rainy   ◯ Foggy   ◯ Humid   ◯ Dry   ◯ Sunny

Kitchen temperature: _____   _Outside temperature:_ _____

_____   _____
YOUR MOOD   YOUR STARTER'S MOOD

_____
STARTER

Amount of starter (in grams): _____   _Amount of leaven, if using (in grams):_ _____

_____
TYPES AND AMOUNTS OF FLOUR (IN GRAMS)

_____
WATER

Temperature: _____   _Total amount of water:_ _____

_____   _____
TOTAL INGREDIENT WEIGHT   IF MULTIPLE LOAVES, WEIGHT OF EACH

TIME OF AUTOLYZE

ADD-INS, IF USED ◯ *Cheese* ◯ *Raisins* ◯ *Seeds* ◯ *Nuts* ◯ *Olives*

RESTING TIME

SALT

KNEADING TIME ◯ *No-Knead Bread*

STRETCHES AND FOLDS

How many folds: _____   *Time between:* _____

QUALITY OF DOUGH ◯ *Sticky* ◯ *Dry* ◯ *Cohesive* ◯ *Soupy* ◯ *Clumpy*

BULK FERMENTATION TIME

SHAPING, APPEARANCE, AND DOUGH TEXTURE BETWEEN STRETCHES AND FOLDS

RISE

SCORING

OVEN TEMPERATURE

BAKING TIME

With lid: _____   *Without lid:* _____

REFRIGERATOR TIME

CRUST COLOR

BAKED LOAF CRUMB

TASTE   ◯ *Sour*   ◯ *Bland*   ◯ *Dry*   ◯ *Gummy*   ◯ *Perfect*

WHO DID YOU GIVE YOUR BREAD TO? WHY?

TO DO DIFFERENTLY NEXT TIME

Turn on your lights before
kneading/incorporating your starter
into the dough. Soon enough
it'll be nighttime and you want to
go to bed, but you have this
dough obligation and you can't do it
in a dim kitchen. You can't.

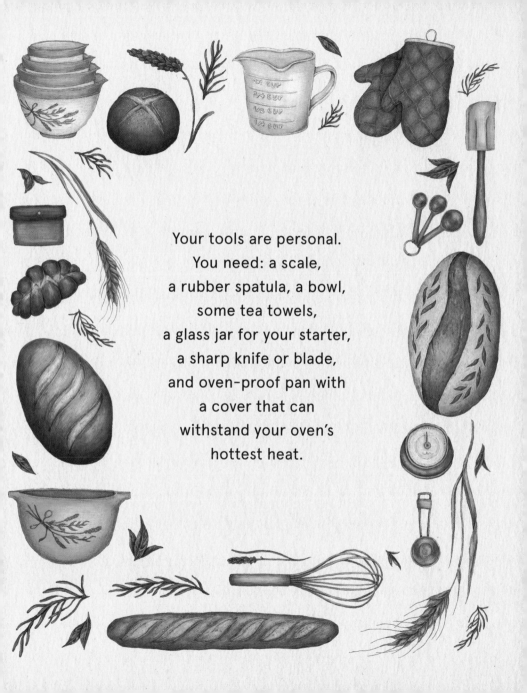

Your tools are personal.
You need: a scale,
a rubber spatula, a bowl,
some tea towels,
a glass jar for your starter,
a sharp knife or blade,
and oven-proof pan with
a cover that can
withstand your oven's
hottest heat.

BREAD LOG

DATE

RECIPE

SEASON ◯ Winter ◯ Spring ◯ Summer ◯ Fall
WEATHER ◯ Rainy ◯ Foggy ◯ Humid ◯ Dry ◯ Sunny

Kitchen temperature: _____

Outside temperature: _____

YOUR MOOD

YOUR STARTER'S MOOD

STARTER

Amount of starter (in grams): _____

Amount of leaven, if using (in grams): _____

TYPES AND AMOUNTS OF FLOUR (IN GRAMS)

WATER

Temperature: _____

Total amount of water: _____

TOTAL INGREDIENT WEIGHT

IF MULTIPLE LOAVES, WEIGHT OF EACH

TIME OF AUTOLYZE

ADD-INS, IF USED ⚪ *Cheese* ⚪ *Raisins* ⚪ *Seeds* ⚪ *Nuts* ⚪ *Olives*

RESTING TIME

SALT

KNEADING TIME ⚪ *No-Knead Bread*

STRETCHES AND FOLDS

How many folds: _____ *Time between:* _____

QUALITY OF DOUGH ⚪ *Sticky* ⚪ *Dry* ⚪ *Cohesive* ⚪ *Soupy* ⚪ *Clumpy*

BULK FERMENTATION TIME

SHAPING, APPEARANCE, AND DOUGH TEXTURE BETWEEN STRETCHES AND FOLDS

RISE

SCORING

OVEN TEMPERATURE

BAKING TIME

With lid: _____   *Without lid:* _____

REFRIGERATOR TIME

CRUST COLOR

BAKED LOAF CRUMB

TASTE ◯ *Sour* ◯ *Bland* ◯ *Dry* ◯ *Gummy* ◯ *Perfect*

WHO DID YOU GIVE YOUR BREAD TO? WHY?

TO DO DIFFERENTLY NEXT TIME

BREAD LOG

DATE

RECIPE

SEASON   ◯ *Winter*   ◯ *Spring*   ◯ *Summer* ◯ *Fall*

WEATHER ◯ *Rainy*   ◯ *Foggy*   ◯ *Humid* ◯ *Dry*   ◯ *Sunny*

Kitchen temperature: _____

Outside temperature: _____

YOUR MOOD

YOUR STARTER'S MOOD

STARTER

Amount of starter (in grams): _____

Amount of leaven, if using (in grams): _____

TYPES AND AMOUNTS OF FLOUR (IN GRAMS)

WATER

Temperature: _____

Total amount of water: _____

TOTAL INGREDIENT WEIGHT

IF MULTIPLE LOAVES, WEIGHT OF EACH

TIME OF AUTOLYZE

ADD-INS, IF USED   ◯ *Cheese*   ◯ *Raisins*   ◯ *Seeds*   ◯ *Nuts*   ◯ *Olives*

RESTING TIME

SALT

KNEADING TIME   ◯ *No-Knead Bread*

STRETCHES AND FOLDS

How many folds: _____   *Time between:* _____

QUALITY OF DOUGH   ◯ *Sticky*   ◯ *Dry*   ◯ *Cohesive*   ◯ *Soupy*   ◯ *Clumpy*

BULK FERMENTATION TIME

SHAPING, APPEARANCE, AND DOUGH TEXTURE BETWEEN STRETCHES AND FOLDS

RISE

SCORING

OVEN TEMPERATURE

BAKING TIME

With lid: _____ *Without lid:* _____

REFRIGERATOR TIME

CRUST COLOR

BAKED LOAF CRUMB

TASTE   ○ *Sour*   ○ *Bland*   ○ *Dry*   ○ *Gummy*   ○ *Perfect*

WHO DID YOU GIVE YOUR BREAD TO? WHY?

TO DO DIFFERENTLY NEXT TIME

BREAD LOG

_____   _____
DATE   RECIPE

SEASON ◯ *Winter* ◯ *Spring* ◯ *Summer* ◯ *Fall*
WEATHER ◯ *Rainy* ◯ *Foggy* ◯ *Humid* ◯ *Dry* ◯ *Sunny*

Kitchen temperature: _____   *Outside temperature:* _____

_____   _____
YOUR MOOD   YOUR STARTER'S MOOD

_____
STARTER

Amount of starter (in grams): _____   *Amount of leaven, if using (in grams):* _____

_____
TYPES AND AMOUNTS OF FLOUR (IN GRAMS)

_____
WATER

Temperature: _____   *Total amount of water:* _____

_____   _____
TOTAL INGREDIENT WEIGHT   IF MULTIPLE LOAVES, WEIGHT OF EACH

TIME OF AUTOLYZE

ADD-INS, IF USED   ◯ *Cheese*   ◯ *Raisins*   ◯ *Seeds*   ◯ *Nuts*   ◯ *Olives*

RESTING TIME

SALT

KNEADING TIME   ◯ *No-Knead Bread*

STRETCHES AND FOLDS

How many folds: _____   *Time between:* _____

QUALITY OF DOUGH   ◯ *Sticky*   ◯ *Dry*   ◯ *Cohesive*   ◯ *Soupy*   ◯ *Clumpy*

BULK FERMENTATION TIME

SHAPING, APPEARANCE, AND DOUGH TEXTURE BETWEEN STRETCHES AND FOLDS

RISE

SCORING

OVEN TEMPERATURE

BAKING TIME

With lid: _____ *Without lid:* _____

REFRIGERATOR TIME

CRUST COLOR

BAKED LOAF CRUMB

TASTE ○ Sour ○ Bland ○ Dry ○ Gummy ○ Perfect

WHO DID YOU GIVE YOUR BREAD TO? WHY?

TO DO DIFFERENTLY NEXT TIME

BREAD LOG

DATE

RECIPE

SEASON ◯ *Winter* ◯ *Spring* ◯ *Summer* ◯ *Fall*

WEATHER ◯ *Rainy* ◯ *Foggy* ◯ *Humid* ◯ *Dry* ◯ *Sunny*

Kitchen temperature: _____

Outside temperature: _____

YOUR MOOD

YOUR STARTER'S MOOD

STARTER

Amount of starter (in grams): _____

Amount of leaven, if using (in grams): _____

TYPES AND AMOUNTS OF FLOUR (IN GRAMS)

WATER

Temperature: _____

Total amount of water: _____

TOTAL INGREDIENT WEIGHT

IF MULTIPLE LOAVES, WEIGHT OF EACH

TIME OF AUTOLYZE

ADD-INS, IF USED ◯ *Cheese* ◯ *Raisins* ◯ *Seeds* ◯ *Nuts* ◯ *Olives*

RESTING TIME

SALT

KNEADING TIME ◯ *No-Knead Bread*

STRETCHES AND FOLDS

How many folds: _____ *Time between:* _____

QUALITY OF DOUGH ◯ *Sticky* ◯ *Dry* ◯ *Cohesive* ◯ *Soupy* ◯ *Clumpy*

BULK FERMENTATION TIME

SHAPING, APPEARANCE, AND DOUGH TEXTURE BETWEEN STRETCHES AND FOLDS

RISE

SCORING

OVEN TEMPERATURE

BAKING TIME

With lid: _____   *Without lid:* _____

REFRIGERATOR TIME

CRUST COLOR

BAKED LOAF CRUMB

TASTE   ◯ *Sour*   ◯ *Bland*   ◯ *Dry*   ◯ *Gummy*   ◯ *Perfect*

WHO DID YOU GIVE YOUR BREAD TO? WHY?

TO DO DIFFERENTLY NEXT TIME

Always keep your sleeves rolled up.
It's annoying to have your
hands deep in dough and deal
with a slipping sleeve.

Do not make bread
while wearing
your favorite sweater.

BREAD LOG

DATE

RECIPE

SEASON   ◯ Winter   ◯ Spring   ◯ Summer   ◯ Fall

WEATHER   ◯ Rainy   ◯ Foggy   ◯ Humid   ◯ Dry   ◯ Sunny

Kitchen temperature: _____

Outside temperature: _____

YOUR MOOD

YOUR STARTER'S MOOD

STARTER

Amount of starter (in grams): _____

Amount of leaven, if using (in grams): _____

TYPES AND AMOUNTS OF FLOUR (IN GRAMS)

WATER

Temperature: _____

Total amount of water: _____

TOTAL INGREDIENT WEIGHT

IF MULTIPLE LOAVES, WEIGHT OF EACH

TIME OF AUTOLYZE

ADD-INS, IF USED ◯ *Cheese* ◯ *Raisins* ◯ *Seeds* ◯ *Nuts* ◯ *Olives*

RESTING TIME

SALT

KNEADING TIME ◯ *No-Knead Bread*

STRETCHES AND FOLDS

How many folds: _____ *Time between:* _____

QUALITY OF DOUGH ◯ *Sticky* ◯ *Dry* ◯ *Cohesive* ◯ *Soupy* ◯ *Clumpy*

BULK FERMENTATION TIME

SHAPING, APPEARANCE, AND DOUGH TEXTURE BETWEEN STRETCHES AND FOLDS

RISE

SCORING

OVEN TEMPERATURE

BAKING TIME

With lid: _____   *Without lid:* _____

REFRIGERATOR TIME

CRUST COLOR

BAKED LOAF CRUMB

TASTE ◯ *Sour* ◯ *Bland* ◯ *Dry* ◯ *Gummy* ◯ *Perfect*

WHO DID YOU GIVE YOUR BREAD TO? WHY?

TO DO DIFFERENTLY NEXT TIME

BREAD LOG

DATE

RECIPE

SEASON   ◯ Winter   ◯ Spring   ◯ Summer   ◯ Fall

WEATHER   ◯ Rainy   ◯ Foggy   ◯ Humid   ◯ Dry   ◯ Sunny

Kitchen temperature: _____

Outside temperature: _____

YOUR MOOD

YOUR STARTER'S MOOD

STARTER

Amount of starter (in grams): _____

Amount of leaven, if using (in grams): _____

TYPES AND AMOUNTS OF FLOUR (IN GRAMS)

WATER

Temperature: _____

Total amount of water: _____

TOTAL INGREDIENT WEIGHT

IF MULTIPLE LOAVES, WEIGHT OF EACH

TIME OF AUTOLYZE

ADD-INS, IF USED   ◯ *Cheese*   ◯ *Raisins*   ◯ *Seeds*   ◯ *Nuts*   ◯ *Olives*

RESTING TIME

SALT

KNEADING TIME   ◯ *No-Knead Bread*

STRETCHES AND FOLDS

How many folds: _____   *Time between:* _____

QUALITY OF DOUGH   ◯ *Sticky*   ◯ *Dry*   ◯ *Cohesive*   ◯ *Soupy*   ◯ *Clumpy*

BULK FERMENTATION TIME

SHAPING, APPEARANCE, AND DOUGH TEXTURE BETWEEN STRETCHES AND FOLDS

RISE

SCORING

OVEN TEMPERATURE

BAKING TIME

With lid: _____   *Without lid:* _____

REFRIGERATOR TIME

CRUST COLOR

BAKED LOAF CRUMB

TASTE ◯ *Sour* ◯ *Bland* ◯ *Dry* ◯ *Gummy* ◯ *Perfect*

WHO DID YOU GIVE YOUR BREAD TO? WHY?

TO DO DIFFERENTLY NEXT TIME

BREAD LOG

DATE

RECIPE

SEASON ◯ Winter ◯ Spring ◯ Summer ◯ Fall
WEATHER ◯ Rainy ◯ Foggy ◯ Humid ◯ Dry ◯ Sunny

Kitchen temperature: _____

Outside temperature: _____

YOUR MOOD

YOUR STARTER'S MOOD

STARTER

Amount of starter (in grams): _____

Amount of leaven, if using (in grams): _____

TYPES AND AMOUNTS OF FLOUR (IN GRAMS)

WATER

Temperature: _____

Total amount of water: _____

TOTAL INGREDIENT WEIGHT

IF MULTIPLE LOAVES, WEIGHT OF EACH

TIME OF AUTOLYZE

ADD-INS, IF USED   ◯ *Cheese*   ◯ *Raisins*   ◯ *Seeds*   ◯ *Nuts*   ◯ *Olives*

RESTING TIME

SALT

KNEADING TIME   ◯ *No-Knead Bread*

STRETCHES AND FOLDS

How many folds: _____   *Time between:* _____

QUALITY OF DOUGH   ◯ *Sticky*   ◯ *Dry*   ◯ *Cohesive*   ◯ *Soupy*   ◯ *Clumpy*

BULK FERMENTATION TIME

SHAPING, APPEARANCE, AND DOUGH TEXTURE BETWEEN STRETCHES AND FOLDS

RISE

SCORING

OVEN TEMPERATURE

BAKING TIME

With lid: _____   *Without lid:* _____

REFRIGERATOR TIME

CRUST COLOR

BAKED LOAF CRUMB

TASTE   ◯ *Sour*   ◯ *Bland*   ◯ *Dry*   ◯ *Gummy*   ◯ *Perfect*

WHO DID YOU GIVE YOUR BREAD TO? WHY?

TO DO DIFFERENTLY NEXT TIME

BREAD LOG

DATE

RECIPE

SEASON   ◯ *Winter*   ◯ *Spring*   ◯ *Summer*   ◯ *Fall*

WEATHER   ◯ *Rainy*   ◯ *Foggy*   ◯ *Humid*   ◯ *Dry*   ◯ *Sunny*

Kitchen temperature: _____

Outside temperature: _____

YOUR MOOD

YOUR STARTER'S MOOD

STARTER

Amount of starter (in grams): _____

Amount of leaven, if using (in grams): _____

TYPES AND AMOUNTS OF FLOUR (IN GRAMS)

WATER

Temperature: _____

Total amount of water: _____

TOTAL INGREDIENT WEIGHT

IF MULTIPLE LOAVES, WEIGHT OF EACH

TIME OF AUTOLYZE

ADD-INS, IF USED   ◯ *Cheese*   ◯ *Raisins*   ◯ *Seeds*   ◯ *Nuts*   ◯ *Olives*

RESTING TIME

SALT

KNEADING TIME   ◯ *No-Knead Bread*

STRETCHES AND FOLDS

How many folds: _____   *Time between:* _____

QUALITY OF DOUGH   ◯ *Sticky*   ◯ *Dry*   ◯ *Cohesive*   ◯ *Soupy*   ◯ *Clumpy*

BULK FERMENTATION TIME

SHAPING, APPEARANCE, AND DOUGH TEXTURE BETWEEN STRETCHES AND FOLDS

RISE

SCORING

OVEN TEMPERATURE

BAKING TIME

With lid: _____   *Without lid:* _____

REFRIGERATOR TIME

CRUST COLOR

BAKED LOAF CRUMB

TASTE ○ *Sour* ○ *Bland* ○ *Dry* ○ *Gummy* ○ *Perfect*

WHO DID YOU GIVE YOUR BREAD TO? WHY?

TO DO DIFFERENTLY NEXT TIME

Use your fridge when
your plans become more
important than your bread.
The refrigerator is
like a magic pause button.

Fancier tools:
bread baskets, dough scraper.
Double your dough and
give your bread away.
Bread makes the best gift.

BREAD LOG

DATE

RECIPE

SEASON   ◯ *Winter*   ◯ *Spring*   ◯ *Summer*   ◯ *Fall*

WEATHER   ◯ *Rainy*   ◯ *Foggy*   ◯ *Humid*   ◯ *Dry*   ◯ *Sunny*

Kitchen temperature: _____   *Outside temperature:* _____

YOUR MOOD

YOUR STARTER'S MOOD

STARTER

Amount of starter (in grams): _____   *Amount of leaven, if using (in grams):* _____

TYPES AND AMOUNTS OF FLOUR (IN GRAMS)

WATER

Temperature: _____   *Total amount of water:* _____

TOTAL INGREDIENT WEIGHT

IF MULTIPLE LOAVES, WEIGHT OF EACH

TIME OF AUTOLYZE

ADD-INS, IF USED   ◯ *Cheese*   ◯ *Raisins*   ◯ *Seeds*   ◯ *Nuts*   ◯ *Olives*

RESTING TIME

SALT

KNEADING TIME   ◯ *No-Knead Bread*

STRETCHES AND FOLDS

How many folds: _____   *Time between:* _____

QUALITY OF DOUGH   ◯ *Sticky*   ◯ *Dry*   ◯ *Cohesive*   ◯ *Soupy*   ◯ *Clumpy*

BULK FERMENTATION TIME

SHAPING, APPEARANCE, AND DOUGH TEXTURE BETWEEN STRETCHES AND FOLDS

RISE

SCORING

OVEN TEMPERATURE

BAKING TIME

With lid: _____   *Without lid:* _____

REFRIGERATOR TIME

CRUST COLOR

BAKED LOAF CRUMB

TASTE   ◯ *Sour*   ◯ *Bland*   ◯ *Dry*   ◯ *Gummy*   ◯ *Perfect*

WHO DID YOU GIVE YOUR BREAD TO? WHY?

TO DO DIFFERENTLY NEXT TIME

BREAD LOG

DATE

RECIPE

SEASON   ◯ *Winter*   ◯ *Spring*   ◯ *Summer*   ◯ *Fall*

WEATHER   ◯ *Rainy*   ◯ *Foggy*   ◯ *Humid*   ◯ *Dry*   ◯ *Sunny*

Kitchen temperature: _____

Outside temperature: _____

YOUR MOOD

YOUR STARTER'S MOOD

STARTER

Amount of starter (in grams): _____

Amount of leaven, if using (in grams): _____

TYPES AND AMOUNTS OF FLOUR (IN GRAMS)

WATER

Temperature: _____

Total amount of water: _____

TOTAL INGREDIENT WEIGHT

IF MULTIPLE LOAVES, WEIGHT OF EACH

TIME OF AUTOLYZE

ADD-INS, IF USED ◯ *Cheese* ◯ *Raisins* ◯ *Seeds* ◯ *Nuts* ◯ *Olives*

RESTING TIME

SALT

KNEADING TIME ◯ *No-Knead Bread*

STRETCHES AND FOLDS

How many folds: _____ *Time between:* _____

QUALITY OF DOUGH ◯ *Sticky* ◯ *Dry* ◯ *Cohesive* ◯ *Soupy* ◯ *Clumpy*

BULK FERMENTATION TIME

SHAPING, APPEARANCE, AND DOUGH TEXTURE BETWEEN STRETCHES AND FOLDS

RISE

SCORING

OVEN TEMPERATURE

BAKING TIME

With lid: _____   *Without lid:* _____

REFRIGERATOR TIME

CRUST COLOR

BAKED LOAF CRUMB

TASTE ◯ *Sour* ◯ *Bland* ◯ *Dry* ◯ *Gummy* ◯ *Perfect*

WHO DID YOU GIVE YOUR BREAD TO? WHY?

TO DO DIFFERENTLY NEXT TIME

BREAD LOG

DATE _____

RECIPE _____

SEASON   ◯ *Winter*   ◯ *Spring*   ◯ *Summer*   ◯ *Fall*

WEATHER   ◯ *Rainy*   ◯ *Foggy*   ◯ *Humid*   ◯ *Dry*   ◯ *Sunny*

Kitchen temperature: _____

Outside temperature: _____

YOUR MOOD _____

YOUR STARTER'S MOOD _____

STARTER

Amount of starter (in grams): _____

Amount of leaven, if using (in grams): _____

TYPES AND AMOUNTS OF FLOUR (IN GRAMS)

WATER

Temperature: _____

Total amount of water: _____

TOTAL INGREDIENT WEIGHT

IF MULTIPLE LOAVES, WEIGHT OF EACH

TIME OF AUTOLYZE

ADD-INS, IF USED   ◯ *Cheese*   ◯ *Raisins*   ◯ *Seeds*   ◯ *Nuts*   ◯ *Olives*

RESTING TIME

SALT

KNEADING TIME   ◯ *No-Knead Bread*

STRETCHES AND FOLDS

How many folds: _____   *Time between:* _____

QUALITY OF DOUGH   ◯ *Sticky*   ◯ *Dry*   ◯ *Cohesive*   ◯ *Soupy*   ◯ *Clumpy*

BULK FERMENTATION TIME

SHAPING, APPEARANCE, AND DOUGH TEXTURE BETWEEN STRETCHES AND FOLDS

RISE

SCORING

OVEN TEMPERATURE

BAKING TIME

With lid: _____   *Without lid:* _____

REFRIGERATOR TIME

CRUST COLOR

BAKED LOAF CRUMB

TASTE   ◯ *Sour*   ◯ *Bland*   ◯ *Dry*   ◯ *Gummy*   ◯ *Perfect*

WHO DID YOU GIVE YOUR BREAD TO? WHY?

TO DO DIFFERENTLY NEXT TIME

Ask each baker you know for a tip,
and combine them to
customize your own patchwork
quilt of a bread recipe.

Watch a lot of shaping videos
on social media.

Cheat on your
favorite bread recipe
and come back
to it smelling different.

BREAD LOG

_____   _____
DATE   RECIPE

SEASON   ◯ Winter ◯ Spring ◯ Summer ◯ Fall
WEATHER ◯ Rainy   ◯ Foggy   ◯ Humid   ◯ Dry   ◯ Sunny

Kitchen temperature: _____   *Outside temperature:* _____

_____   _____
YOUR MOOD   YOUR STARTER'S MOOD

_____
STARTER

Amount of starter (in grams): _____   *Amount of leaven, if using (in grams):* _____

_____
TYPES AND AMOUNTS OF FLOUR (IN GRAMS)

_____
WATER

Temperature: _____   *Total amount of water:* _____

_____   _____
TOTAL INGREDIENT WEIGHT   IF MULTIPLE LOAVES, WEIGHT OF EACH

TIME OF AUTOLYZE

ADD-INS, IF USED ○ *Cheese* ○ *Raisins* ○ *Seeds* ○ *Nuts* ○ *Olives*

RESTING TIME

SALT

KNEADING TIME ○ *No-Knead Bread*

STRETCHES AND FOLDS

How many folds: _____ *Time between:* _____

QUALITY OF DOUGH ○ *Sticky* ○ *Dry* ○ *Cohesive* ○ *Soupy* ○ *Clumpy*

BULK FERMENTATION TIME

SHAPING, APPEARANCE, AND DOUGH TEXTURE BETWEEN STRETCHES AND FOLDS

RISE

SCORING

OVEN TEMPERATURE

BAKING TIME

With lid: _____   *Without lid:* _____

REFRIGERATOR TIME

CRUST COLOR

BAKED LOAF CRUMB

TASTE   ◯ *Sour*   ◯ *Bland*   ◯ *Dry*   ◯ *Gummy*   ◯ *Perfect*

WHO DID YOU GIVE YOUR BREAD TO? WHY?

TO DO DIFFERENTLY NEXT TIME

BREAD LOG

DATE

RECIPE

SEASON   ◯ *Winter*   ◯ *Spring*   ◯ *Summer*   ◯ *Fall*

WEATHER   ◯ *Rainy*   ◯ *Foggy*   ◯ *Humid*   ◯ *Dry*   ◯ *Sunny*

Kitchen temperature: _____

Outside temperature: _____

YOUR MOOD

YOUR STARTER'S MOOD

STARTER

Amount of starter (in grams): _____

Amount of leaven, if using (in grams): _____

TYPES AND AMOUNTS OF FLOUR (IN GRAMS)

WATER

Temperature: _____

Total amount of water: _____

TOTAL INGREDIENT WEIGHT

IF MULTIPLE LOAVES, WEIGHT OF EACH

TIME OF AUTOLYZE

ADD-INS, IF USED   ◯ *Cheese*   ◯ *Raisins*   ◯ *Seeds*   ◯ *Nuts*   ◯ *Olives*

RESTING TIME

SALT

KNEADING TIME   ◯ *No-Knead Bread*

STRETCHES AND FOLDS

How many folds: _____   *Time between:* _____

QUALITY OF DOUGH   ◯ *Sticky*   ◯ *Dry*   ◯ *Cohesive*   ◯ *Soupy*   ◯ *Clumpy*

BULK FERMENTATION TIME

SHAPING, APPEARANCE, AND DOUGH TEXTURE BETWEEN STRETCHES AND FOLDS

RISE

SCORING

OVEN TEMPERATURE

BAKING TIME

With lid: _____   *Without lid:* _____

REFRIGERATOR TIME

CRUST COLOR

BAKED LOAF CRUMB

TASTE   ◯ *Sour*   ◯ *Bland*   ◯ *Dry*   ◯ *Gummy*   ◯ *Perfect*

WHO DID YOU GIVE YOUR BREAD TO? WHY?

TO DO DIFFERENTLY NEXT TIME

BREAD LOG

DATE

RECIPE

SEASON ○ Winter ○ Spring ○ Summer ○ Fall
WEATHER ○ Rainy ○ Foggy ○ Humid ○ Dry ○ Sunny

Kitchen temperature: _____

Outside temperature: _____

YOUR MOOD

YOUR STARTER'S MOOD

STARTER

Amount of starter (in grams): _____

Amount of leaven, if using (in grams): _____

TYPES AND AMOUNTS OF FLOUR (IN GRAMS)

WATER

Temperature: _____

Total amount of water: _____

TOTAL INGREDIENT WEIGHT

IF MULTIPLE LOAVES, WEIGHT OF EACH

TIME OF AUTOLYZE

ADD-INS, IF USED   ◯ *Cheese*   ◯ *Raisins*   ◯ *Seeds*   ◯ *Nuts*   ◯ *Olives*

RESTING TIME

SALT

KNEADING TIME   ◯ *No-Knead Bread*

STRETCHES AND FOLDS

How many folds: _____   *Time between:* _____

QUALITY OF DOUGH   ◯ *Sticky*   ◯ *Dry*   ◯ *Cohesive*   ◯ *Soupy*   ◯ *Clumpy*

BULK FERMENTATION TIME

SHAPING, APPEARANCE, AND DOUGH TEXTURE BETWEEN STRETCHES AND FOLDS

RISE

SCORING

OVEN TEMPERATURE

BAKING TIME

With lid: _____   *Without lid:* _____

REFRIGERATOR TIME

CRUST COLOR

BAKED LOAF CRUMB

TASTE   ◯ *Sour*   ◯ *Bland*   ◯ *Dry*   ◯ *Gummy*   ◯ *Perfect*

WHO DID YOU GIVE YOUR BREAD TO? WHY?

TO DO DIFFERENTLY NEXT TIME

Add the water to your
bread throughout the mixing process
rather than all at once.
This will help keep the flour hydrated.

If you struggle with dissolving
the salt into your dough,
hold back a little of your total water
and add it with the salt.

Squeeze, pull,
push, spank, slap, and
cut the dough.
Going from powder
to a crust is nothing
short of magic.

BREAD LOG

DATE

RECIPE

SEASON ⚪ Winter ⚪ Spring ⚪ Summer ⚪ Fall
WEATHER ⚪ Rainy ⚪ Foggy ⚪ Humid ⚪ Dry ⚪ Sunny

Kitchen temperature: _____

Outside temperature: _____

YOUR MOOD

YOUR STARTER'S MOOD

STARTER

Amount of starter (in grams): _____

Amount of leaven, if using (in grams): _____

TYPES AND AMOUNTS OF FLOUR (IN GRAMS)

WATER

Temperature: _____

Total amount of water: _____

TOTAL INGREDIENT WEIGHT

IF MULTIPLE LOAVES, WEIGHT OF EACH

TIME OF AUTOLYZE

ADD-INS, IF USED   ◯ *Cheese*   ◯ *Raisins*   ◯ *Seeds*   ◯ *Nuts*   ◯ *Olives*

RESTING TIME

SALT

KNEADING TIME   ◯ *No-Knead Bread*

STRETCHES AND FOLDS

How many folds: _____   *Time between:* _____

QUALITY OF DOUGH   ◯ *Sticky*   ◯ *Dry*   ◯ *Cohesive*   ◯ *Soupy*   ◯ *Clumpy*

BULK FERMENTATION TIME

SHAPING, APPEARANCE, AND DOUGH TEXTURE BETWEEN STRETCHES AND FOLDS

RISE

SCORING

OVEN TEMPERATURE

BAKING TIME

With lid: _____   *Without lid:* _____

REFRIGERATOR TIME

CRUST COLOR

BAKED LOAF CRUMB

TASTE ○ *Sour* ○ *Bland* ○ *Dry* ○ *Gummy* ○ *Perfect*

WHO DID YOU GIVE YOUR BREAD TO? WHY?

TO DO DIFFERENTLY NEXT TIME

BREAD LOG

DATE

RECIPE

SEASON ○ Winter ○ Spring ○ Summer ○ Fall
WEATHER ○ Rainy ○ Foggy ○ Humid ○ Dry ○ Sunny

Kitchen temperature: _____

Outside temperature: _____

YOUR MOOD

YOUR STARTER'S MOOD

STARTER

Amount of starter (in grams): _____

Amount of leaven, if using (in grams): _____

TYPES AND AMOUNTS OF FLOUR (IN GRAMS)

WATER

Temperature: _____

Total amount of water: _____

TOTAL INGREDIENT WEIGHT

IF MULTIPLE LOAVES, WEIGHT OF EACH

TIME OF AUTOLYZE

ADD-INS, IF USED   ◯ *Cheese*   ◯ *Raisins*   ◯ *Seeds*   ◯ *Nuts*   ◯ *Olives*

RESTING TIME

SALT

KNEADING TIME   ◯ *No-Knead Bread*

STRETCHES AND FOLDS

How many folds: _____   *Time between:* _____

QUALITY OF DOUGH   ◯ *Sticky*   ◯ *Dry*   ◯ *Cohesive*   ◯ *Soupy*   ◯ *Clumpy*

BULK FERMENTATION TIME

SHAPING, APPEARANCE, AND DOUGH TEXTURE BETWEEN STRETCHES AND FOLDS

RISE

SCORING

OVEN TEMPERATURE

BAKING TIME

With lid: _____ *Without lid:* _____

REFRIGERATOR TIME

CRUST COLOR

BAKED LOAF CRUMB

TASTE ○ Sour ○ Bland ○ Dry ○ Gummy ○ Perfect

WHO DID YOU GIVE YOUR BREAD TO? WHY?

TO DO DIFFERENTLY NEXT TIME

BREAD LOG

DATE _____

RECIPE _____

SEASON ◯ *Winter* ◯ *Spring* ◯ *Summer* ◯ *Fall*

WEATHER ◯ *Rainy* ◯ *Foggy* ◯ *Humid* ◯ *Dry* ◯ *Sunny*

Kitchen temperature: _____

Outside temperature: _____

YOUR MOOD

YOUR STARTER'S MOOD

STARTER

Amount of starter (in grams): _____

Amount of leaven, if using (in grams): _____

TYPES AND AMOUNTS OF FLOUR (IN GRAMS)

WATER

Temperature: _____

Total amount of water: _____

TOTAL INGREDIENT WEIGHT

IF MULTIPLE LOAVES, WEIGHT OF EACH

TIME OF AUTOLYZE

ADD-INS, IF USED ◯ *Cheese* ◯ *Raisins* ◯ *Seeds* ◯ *Nuts* ◯ *Olives*

RESTING TIME

SALT

KNEADING TIME ◯ *No-Knead Bread*

STRETCHES AND FOLDS

How many folds: _____ *Time between:* _____

QUALITY OF DOUGH ◯ *Sticky* ◯ *Dry* ◯ *Cohesive* ◯ *Soupy* ◯ *Clumpy*

BULK FERMENTATION TIME

SHAPING, APPEARANCE, AND DOUGH TEXTURE BETWEEN STRETCHES AND FOLDS

RISE

SCORING

OVEN TEMPERATURE

BAKING TIME

With lid: _____   *Without lid:* _____

REFRIGERATOR TIME

CRUST COLOR

BAKED LOAF CRUMB

TASTE   ◯ *Sour*   ◯ *Bland*   ◯ *Dry*   ◯ *Gummy*   ◯ *Perfect*

WHO DID YOU GIVE YOUR BREAD TO? WHY?

TO DO DIFFERENTLY NEXT TIME

Your hands are a great indicator
of how your bread is doing.
When your dough is too sticky, you
will see it on your hands.

If you wet your hands first,
handling your dough at any stage
will be easier, and you
will be pulling less dough off your
hands when it's time to stop.

If your bread
goes stale, save it for
French toast,
croutons, or panzanella,
or grind it up
for breadcrumbs.

BREAD LOG

DATE

RECIPE

SEASON ⚪ Winter ⚪ Spring ⚪ Summer ⚪ Fall

WEATHER ⚪ Rainy ⚪ Foggy ⚪ Humid ⚪ Dry ⚪ Sunny

Kitchen temperature: _____

Outside temperature: _____

YOUR MOOD

YOUR STARTER'S MOOD

STARTER

Amount of starter (in grams): _____

Amount of leaven, if using (in grams): _____

TYPES AND AMOUNTS OF FLOUR (IN GRAMS)

WATER

Temperature: _____

Total amount of water: _____

TOTAL INGREDIENT WEIGHT

IF MULTIPLE LOAVES, WEIGHT OF EACH

TIME OF AUTOLYZE

ADD-INS, IF USED   ◯ *Cheese*   ◯ *Raisins*   ◯ *Seeds*   ◯ *Nuts*   ◯ *Olives*

RESTING TIME

SALT

KNEADING TIME   ◯ *No-Knead Bread*

STRETCHES AND FOLDS

How many folds: _____   *Time between:* _____

QUALITY OF DOUGH   ◯ *Sticky*   ◯ *Dry*   ◯ *Cohesive*   ◯ *Soupy*   ◯ *Clumpy*

BULK FERMENTATION TIME

SHAPING, APPEARANCE, AND DOUGH TEXTURE BETWEEN STRETCHES AND FOLDS

RISE

SCORING

OVEN TEMPERATURE

BAKING TIME

With lid: _____   *Without lid:* _____

REFRIGERATOR TIME

CRUST COLOR

BAKED LOAF CRUMB

TASTE   ◯ Sour   ◯ Bland   ◯ Dry   ◯ Gummy   ◯ Perfect

WHO DID YOU GIVE YOUR BREAD TO? WHY?

TO DO DIFFERENTLY NEXT TIME

BREAD LOG

DATE

RECIPE

SEASON ○ Winter ○ Spring ○ Summer ○ Fall
WEATHER ○ Rainy ○ Foggy ○ Humid ○ Dry ○ Sunny

Kitchen temperature: _____

Outside temperature: _____

YOUR MOOD

YOUR STARTER'S MOOD

STARTER

Amount of starter (in grams): _____

Amount of leaven, if using (in grams): _____

TYPES AND AMOUNTS OF FLOUR (IN GRAMS)

WATER

Temperature: _____

Total amount of water: _____

TOTAL INGREDIENT WEIGHT

IF MULTIPLE LOAVES, WEIGHT OF EACH

TIME OF AUTOLYZE

ADD-INS, IF USED ◯ *Cheese* ◯ *Raisins* ◯ *Seeds* ◯ *Nuts* ◯ *Olives*

RESTING TIME

SALT

KNEADING TIME ◯ *No-Knead Bread*

STRETCHES AND FOLDS

How many folds: _____ *Time between:* _____

QUALITY OF DOUGH ◯ *Sticky* ◯ *Dry* ◯ *Cohesive* ◯ *Soupy* ◯ *Clumpy*

BULK FERMENTATION TIME

SHAPING, APPEARANCE, AND DOUGH TEXTURE BETWEEN STRETCHES AND FOLDS

RISE

SCORING

OVEN TEMPERATURE

BAKING TIME

With lid: _____   *Without lid:* _____

REFRIGERATOR TIME

CRUST COLOR

BAKED LOAF CRUMB

TASTE   ◯ *Sour*   ◯ *Bland*   ◯ *Dry*   ◯ *Gummy*   ◯ *Perfect*

WHO DID YOU GIVE YOUR BREAD TO? WHY?

TO DO DIFFERENTLY NEXT TIME

BREAD LOG

DATE

RECIPE

SEASON ◯ Winter ◯ Spring ◯ Summer ◯ Fall
WEATHER ◯ Rainy ◯ Foggy ◯ Humid ◯ Dry ◯ Sunny

Kitchen temperature: _____

Outside temperature: _____

YOUR MOOD

YOUR STARTER'S MOOD

STARTER

Amount of starter (in grams): _____

Amount of leaven, if using (in grams): _____

TYPES AND AMOUNTS OF FLOUR (IN GRAMS)

WATER

Temperature: _____

Total amount of water: _____

TOTAL INGREDIENT WEIGHT

IF MULTIPLE LOAVES, WEIGHT OF EACH

TIME OF AUTOLYZE

ADD-INS, IF USED ◯ *Cheese* ◯ *Raisins* ◯ *Seeds* ◯ *Nuts* ◯ *Olives*

RESTING TIME

SALT

KNEADING TIME ◯ *No-Knead Bread*

STRETCHES AND FOLDS

How many folds: _____ *Time between:* _____

QUALITY OF DOUGH ◯ *Sticky* ◯ *Dry* ◯ *Cohesive* ◯ *Soupy* ◯ *Clumpy*

BULK FERMENTATION TIME

SHAPING, APPEARANCE, AND DOUGH TEXTURE BETWEEN STRETCHES AND FOLDS

RISE

SCORING

OVEN TEMPERATURE

BAKING TIME

With lid: _____   *Without lid:* _____

REFRIGERATOR TIME

CRUST COLOR

BAKED LOAF CRUMB

TASTE   ◯ *Sour*   ◯ *Bland*   ◯ *Dry*   ◯ *Gummy*   ◯ *Perfect*

WHO DID YOU GIVE YOUR BREAD TO? WHY?

TO DO DIFFERENTLY NEXT TIME

Pay attention to how the dough feels against your skin. When the dough is almost vibrating, bubbles form on the dough's surface, and it doesn't stick to you, it's ready to go into the fridge for the night.

Rescue your
sad-looking, soupy
dough by
making focaccia
or flatbread.

BREAD LOG

DATE

RECIPE

SEASON   ◯ Winter   ◯ Spring   ◯ Summer   ◯ Fall

WEATHER   ◯ Rainy   ◯ Foggy   ◯ Humid   ◯ Dry   ◯ Sunny

Kitchen temperature: _____

Outside temperature: _____

YOUR MOOD

YOUR STARTER'S MOOD

STARTER

Amount of starter (in grams): _____

Amount of leaven, if using (in grams): _____

TYPES AND AMOUNTS OF FLOUR (IN GRAMS)

WATER

Temperature: _____

Total amount of water: _____

TOTAL INGREDIENT WEIGHT

IF MULTIPLE LOAVES, WEIGHT OF EACH

TIME OF AUTOLYZE

ADD-INS, IF USED ○ *Cheese* ○ *Raisins* ○ *Seeds* ○ *Nuts* ○ *Olives*

RESTING TIME

SALT

KNEADING TIME ○ *No-Knead Bread*

STRETCHES AND FOLDS

How many folds: _____ *Time between:* _____

QUALITY OF DOUGH ○ *Sticky* ○ *Dry* ○ *Cohesive* ○ *Soupy* ○ *Clumpy*

BULK FERMENTATION TIME

SHAPING, APPEARANCE, AND DOUGH TEXTURE BETWEEN STRETCHES AND FOLDS

RISE

SCORING

OVEN TEMPERATURE

BAKING TIME

With lid: _____   *Without lid:* _____

REFRIGERATOR TIME

CRUST COLOR

BAKED LOAF CRUMB

TASTE   ◯ *Sour*   ◯ *Bland*   ◯ *Dry*   ◯ *Gummy*   ◯ *Perfect*

WHO DID YOU GIVE YOUR BREAD TO? WHY?

TO DO DIFFERENTLY NEXT TIME

BREAD LOG

DATE

RECIPE

SEASON ◯ *Winter* ◯ *Spring* ◯ *Summer* ◯ *Fall*

WEATHER ◯ *Rainy* ◯ *Foggy* ◯ *Humid* ◯ *Dry* ◯ *Sunny*

Kitchen temperature: _____

Outside temperature: _____

YOUR MOOD

YOUR STARTER'S MOOD

STARTER

Amount of starter (in grams): _____

Amount of leaven, if using (in grams): _____

TYPES AND AMOUNTS OF FLOUR (IN GRAMS)

WATER

Temperature: _____

Total amount of water: _____

TOTAL INGREDIENT WEIGHT

IF MULTIPLE LOAVES, WEIGHT OF EACH

TIME OF AUTOLYZE

ADD-INS, IF USED ○ *Cheese*   ○ *Raisins*   ○ *Seeds*   ○ *Nuts*   ○ *Olives*

RESTING TIME

SALT

KNEADING TIME   ○ *No-Knead Bread*

STRETCHES AND FOLDS

How many folds: _____   *Time between:* _____

QUALITY OF DOUGH   ○ *Sticky*   ○ *Dry*   ○ *Cohesive*   ○ *Soupy*   ○ *Clumpy*

BULK FERMENTATION TIME

SHAPING, APPEARANCE, AND DOUGH TEXTURE BETWEEN STRETCHES AND FOLDS

RISE

SCORING

OVEN TEMPERATURE

BAKING TIME

With lid: _____   *Without lid:* _____

REFRIGERATOR TIME

CRUST COLOR

BAKED LOAF CRUMB

TASTE   ◯ *Sour*   ◯ *Bland*   ◯ *Dry*   ◯ *Gummy*   ◯ *Perfect*

WHO DID YOU GIVE YOUR BREAD TO? WHY?

TO DO DIFFERENTLY NEXT TIME

BREAD LOG

_____   _____
DATE   RECIPE

_____
SEASON   ◯ Winter   ◯ Spring   ◯ Summer   ◯ Fall
WEATHER   ◯ Rainy   ◯ Foggy   ◯ Humid   ◯ Dry   ◯ Sunny

Kitchen temperature: _____   *Outside temperature:* _____

_____   _____
YOUR MOOD   YOUR STARTER'S MOOD

_____
STARTER

Amount of starter (in grams): _____   *Amount of leaven, if using (in grams):* _____

_____
TYPES AND AMOUNTS OF FLOUR (IN GRAMS)

_____
WATER

Temperature: _____   *Total amount of water:* _____

_____   _____
TOTAL INGREDIENT WEIGHT   IF MULTIPLE LOAVES, WEIGHT OF EACH

TIME OF AUTOLYZE

ADD-INS, IF USED   ◯ *Cheese*   ◯ *Raisins*   ◯ *Seeds*   ◯ *Nuts*   ◯ *Olives*

RESTING TIME

SALT

KNEADING TIME   ◯ *No-Knead Bread*

STRETCHES AND FOLDS

How many folds: _____   *Time between:* _____

QUALITY OF DOUGH   ◯ *Sticky*   ◯ *Dry*   ◯ *Cohesive*   ◯ *Soupy*   ◯ *Clumpy*

BULK FERMENTATION TIME

SHAPING, APPEARANCE, AND DOUGH TEXTURE BETWEEN STRETCHES AND FOLDS

RISE

SCORING

OVEN TEMPERATURE

BAKING TIME

With lid: _____   *Without lid:* _____

REFRIGERATOR TIME

CRUST COLOR

BAKED LOAF CRUMB

TASTE ○ *Sour* ○ *Bland* ○ *Dry* ○ *Gummy* ○ *Perfect*

WHO DID YOU GIVE YOUR BREAD TO? WHY?

TO DO DIFFERENTLY NEXT TIME

Clean your tools, hands,
and workspace often when you are
working with dough. And empty
your sink of dishes before you start.
When you wash your hands or
your bowls atop your dirty dishes,
the dough will make its way
onto everything.

A wire scrub brush is
a useful tool for cleaning
up the stickiness.

RESOURCES

The internet is full of bakers and resources. It's an excellent place to learn about bread. Some bakers are particularly generous with their advice and time.

BAKERS:

Alchemy Bread
alchemybread.com
@alchemybread

Artisan Bryan
artisanbryan.com
@artisanbryan

Challenger Breadware
challengerbreadware.com
*a great pan that will take your bread
to the next level*

Elaine Boddy
foodbodsourdough.com
@elaine_foodbod

Full Proof Baking
@fullproofbaking

King Arthur Baking Company
kingarthurbaking.com
*King Arthur has a bread hotline
with dedicated bakers who can help
you fix your browned bottoms,
over-under-proofed conundrums,
and starter woes*

**Mark Bittman's
No-Knead Bread**
https://cooking.nytimes.com/
recipes/11376-no-knead-bread

Maurizio Leo
The Perfect Loaf
theperfectloaf.com
@maurizio

Tara Jenson
Baker Hands
@bakerhands

Trevor Wilson
Breadwerx
breadwerx.com
@trevorjaywilson
*Trevor Wilson of Breadwerx has a
great sourdough he calls Champlain.
I made this loaf again and again,
really liked the flavor, so applied his
proportions of spelt, rye, and bread
flour to my regular loaf.*

DIRECT-SHIP MILLERS:

Central Milling
centralmilling.com

Farmer Ground Flour
farmergroundflour.com

Maine Grains
Skowhegan, Maine
mainegrains.com

Migrash Flour
Maryland
migrashfarm.com

SOURDOUGH
DISCARD RECIPES:

Bryan Ford
Artisan Bryan
https://www.artisanbryan.com/
sourdough-discard-recipes

King Arthur Baking Company
https://www.kingarthurbaking.
com/recipes/collections/
sourdough-discard-recipes

Maurizio Leo
The Perfect Loaf
https://www.theperfectloaf.com/
my-top-3-leftover-sourdough-
starter-recipes/

Princeton Architectural Press
202 Warren Street, Hudson, NY 12534
www.papress.com

© 2021 Princeton Architectural Press
All rights reserved
No part of this book may be used or reproduced in
any manner without written permission from the publisher,
except in the case of reviews.

ISBN 978-1-64896-005-5
Manufactured in China
10 9 8 7 6 5 4 3 2 1

EDITOR: Sara McKay
ILLUSTRATIONS BY Jessica Roux
TEXT BY Sarah Raymont
DESIGNERS: Natalie Snodgrass, Paul Wagner